Original title:
Bloom Where You're Potted

Copyright © 2025 Creative Arts Management OÜ
All rights reserved.

Author: Eleanor Prescott
ISBN HARDBACK: 978-1-80581-729-1
ISBN PAPERBACK: 978-1-80581-256-2
ISBN EBOOK: 978-1-80581-729-1

Against the Grain

In a tiny pot, I wiggle and sway,
Got roots so strong, I won't decay.
You call me stubborn, I call it flair,
Dancing with weeds? I'm beyond compare.

Sunflower talks, they brag and boast,
But in my corner, I'm the host.
Chasing light like a cat with string,
Proud of my pot, I'm the weirdest thing.

Petals in the Dust

Dusty roads are where I thrive,
Petals messy, but I'm alive.
In a corner from some clown's show,
I sip on rain and steal the glow.

You won't find me in gardens grand,
I'm partying on a sidewalk stand.
Each passerby, a laugh, a joke,
I throw a party with every poke.

The Will to Wonder

Who's that looking, tall and wide?
Oh, it's me, your potting pride!
With every glimpse, I've got a wink,
A flower in plaid, what do you think?

I stretch my leaves for all to see,
Wondering if there's more to be.
A bee passes by, gives me a nudge,
I'll pose for selfies, I won't budge!

Sow Hope in Concrete

Cracks in concrete, my cozy bed,
Planting dreams, that's how I spread.
Chasing those rays with a goofy grin,
A weed in a suit? Well, let's begin!

Sow my hopes where no one dares,
Shaking my leaves, I'm full of airs.
If life gives you grit, dance like mad,
In this little pot, I'm truly glad!

The Art of Flourishing

In a corner, I find my place,
Sunlight's warm, I'm in the race.
With a leaf here and a sprout there,
Why not grow? I have flair!

Neighbors sigh, and plants get tall,
I'll just laugh, having a ball.
With tiny roots, I stretch and sway,
Who knew small could steal the day!

Sprout from the Shadows

Dancing light, a sneak peek wait,
I'll thrive here, isn't that great?
In the dark, I wiggle about,
Planting joy, there's no doubt.

When they all think I can't win,
I giggle, let the fun begin!
I soak up what I can, just right,
Watch me grow, oh, what a sight!

Resilience in a Tiny Pot

Stuck in this cup, feeling tight,
Yet my spirit's taking flight.
With every sip of morning dew,
I'll make this pot a lively zoo!

While others boast in gardens wide,
I'll thrive here, full of pride.
A crunched-up leaf, no big deal,
My laughs, you know, will steal the meal!

The Dance of Survival

In a window, I twist and twirl,
Oh yes, I'm the life of this whirl!
With each gust that comes to play,
I sway like it's a sunny day.

A little rain makes me sprightly bright,
I'll shimmy through the day and night.
With roots that wiggle, never shy,
Let's have a party, oh my, oh my!

Roots Beneath the Surface

In a pot so small, I wiggle my toes,
Making friends with the worms, nobody knows.
I dance with the soil, a wiggly cheer,
While dreaming of gardens, far from here.

My roots stretch wide, like a party gone wild,
Shouting at daisies, I'm the funky child.
No room for a frown, I'll find my own groove,
In the land of the pots, I've got nothing to prove.

Resilience in a Tiny Space

In this tiny cage, I'm a wild, wacky sight,
Throwing shade on the sun, I shine so bright.
With leaves like umbrellas, I block out the rain,
Making jokes with the bugs, oh what a pain!

Said the little plant, 'I can't be contained!'
With a wink and a grin, no rules to be gained.
I twist and I bend, like a dancer on stage,
In my pocket-sized world, I'm ready to rage.

Thrive Against the Odds

With a sip of my water, I giggle and grow,
While the critters all watch with a snicker and 'whoa!'
A sprout with a dream, I'm a fearless delight,
Outshining the stars with my quirky plant height.

They say it's too shady, they say it's too tight,
But I've got my moves, and I'm ready to fight.
Like a champ in the ring, I'll stand my own ground,
Who knew a small pot could feel so profound?

Beauty in Boundaries

Stacked high like a tower, here I stand tall,
Making friends with the fence, we're having a ball.
In this cozy corner, I spin tales of dreams,
With petals so funny, bursting at the seams.

Said the sprout to the stone, 'Let's throw a soirée!'
With laughter and colors, come dance, come play.
In a world full of limits, I toast with a cheer,
Finding joy in this pot, nothing left to fear!

Nature's Hidden Triumphs

In a cracked pot, a daisy sneezes,
It giggles in wind, sways with breezes.
A cactus wears sunglasses, bright and bold,
Thinks it's a beachgoer, or so I'm told.

A fern in the corner, feeling quite grand,
Practices yoga, it's well in demand.
While weeds throw parties, oh what a sight,
Dance to the sound of the garden's delight.

Thorns and Tenderness

A rose with thorns, it tells a bad joke,
Says life's too short for a prickly cloak.
The tulip laughs, for it doesn't feel pain,
It fluffs its petals, dances in the rain.

A dandelion whispers, "Life's such a breeze,
I float above troubles, just doing as I please."
With a wink and a puff, it scatters its seeds,
Sowing laughter in cracks, fulfilling its needs.

Unveiling Potential

A little sprout thinks it's a big tree,
Swaying and posing, full of glee.
A sunflower dreams of a movie star,
Wishing on beams from Jupiter, not far.

The plants in the garden gossip away,
Arguing who'd win if they played tag each day.
While the herbs concoct a secretive plot,
To spice up the world, with laughs, they've got.

Striving for the Sun

A tiny sprig stretches, reaching for rays,
It's determined to shine, in oh-so-many ways.
A petunia with flair, considers a strut,
It's all about style, in its little rut.

A dahlia argues, "I've got the best hue!"
While daisies compete for who's freshest and new.
They giggle and wiggle, full of delight,
In a world of potting, it's a colorful fight.

The Rise of Color in the Gloom

In a world that's gray and dull,
I wear my socks all mismatched,
Dancing in the kitchen light,
I'm the rainbow, they're the catch.

Paint the walls with laughter loud,
This chair's my throne, I feel so proud,
With a mug that says 'World's Best',
I sip my tea and jest, jest, jest!

Who needs a garden, I've got flair,
A plant that thrives on total despair,
Its leaves are shiny, not a care,
We laugh at gloom, a perfect pair!

So here's to life, a vibrant jest,
In the mess, we're truly blessed,
Find your color, make it pop,
In every corner, laughter won't stop!

Wildflowers of the Unconventional

Caught in the cracks of city streets,
I'm a daisy, not a rose,
Waving arms where no one greets,
With my roots in funny prose.

Wearing sneakers on a night out,
My hair, a bird's nest wild and free,
Who says the weeds can't show some clout?
Watch me dance, not on decree!

A bees' delight, a curious sight,
Buzzing past, they take a look,
Wildflower hearts are pure delight,
Writing life's great funny book!

So here's to us, the quirky crew,
Painting gardens in a rush,
Unconventional, we laugh anew,
With wisdom found in every blush!

The Beauty of Unexpected Places

In a crack by the garbage bin,
A flower blooms with style and grace,
Neighbors stare, and then they grin,
At nature's wild, unexpected place.

Right between dumpsters, bright and bold,
It waves like it's got big dreams,
With petals that are laced in gold,
Nothing is quite as it seems!

A soft breeze carries jokes galore,
As pigeons coo in playful glee,
Who needs a stage? I'm here for more,
At odd spots, I feel so free!

So let the world roll its eyes,
As I thrive in the oddest nook,
Life's a surprise in every guise,
Watch me shine—I'm off the hook!

Finding Freedom in Limits

Boxed in tight, I start to dance,
A hula hoop around my waist,
With every spin, I find my chance,
To laugh at fate, I'm feeling braced.

When life's confined, unleash the fun,
I juggle dreams, a comedy act,
Though my pot feels small, I run,
With joy that's fierce and intact!

A lid on a jar cannot contain,
The wild adventures in my mind,
In every limit, there's a gain,
My spirit's free, no bind to find!

So here's to those who break the mold,
In gardens small, the heart can soar,
Embrace the weird, be brave, be bold,
In little pots, we'll find much more!

Nurtured in Harsh Environments

In a pot so small and tight,
I dance in the morning light.
With weeds for friends and bugs for foes,
I wear my thorns like snazzy clothes.

Though the soil is rough and dry,
I reach for the bright blue sky.
My roots are tangled, what a mess!
But watch me strut, I must confess.

Sometimes I get a little frazzled,
With every wind, I'm quite bedazzled.
But sunshine makes me feel alive,
In this funky pot, I thrive and jive.

When raindrops fall, I throw a party,
Invite the ants: they bring the hearty!
In a world that's cramped and tight,
I'll grow with all my quirky might.

Blossoms of Hope

In the corner of the room, I smile,
Cramped but cute, I make it worthwhile.
With laughter echoing all around,
My petals dance, oh what a sound!

The cat thinks I'm a tasty snack,
But I'm too sassy to hold back.
I flash my colors, bright and bold,
A tiny miracle to behold.

Every drop of water's a delight,
I stretch my leaves, reaching for height.
Neighbors grumble, 'What a sight!'
But I'm the star of this pot of light.

In this pot, I'm never sore,
Each day I promise, there's more in store.
I might be small, but my dreams are grand,
As I spread joy, in this little land.

Finding Light in Limited Space

A sunny spot, but just a sliver,
I twist and turn, oh how I quiver!
With chores galore, I'm on a quest,
To find the light, I'll do my best.

A hungry spider stopped for tea,
He spun a web, just to tease me.
With each webbed corner, I must plot,
Hey! That's my leaf; you silly tot!

I stretch out wide; it's quite the show!
While chatting with the grass below.
'We'll make this place a cozy nest,'
I say with pride, 'We are the best.'

Laughter here, and jokes galore,
In this alight space, who could want more?
So here I sit, a vibrant spree,
Finding joy where it seems not to be.

Petals of Perseverance

In a pot with no room to roam,
I've claimed my throne, it's quite my home.
Though others wilt at every glance,
I shimmy and shake; I love to dance.

Dust bunnies visit, oh what a sight,
They whisper secrets of brave delight.
I laugh aloud at the absurd,
Grateful for every little word.

Through leaks and spills, I stand so proud,
While housemates grumble, I sing loud.
It's not the size that makes me thrive,
It's the spirit that keeps me alive.

So here I sway in my tiny space,
With petals bright, I join the race.
In every struggle, I find my cheer,
With petals of perseverance, I'm here!

Dance of the Daring Flora

In a corner, there's a sprout,
Doing the cha-cha, without a doubt.
Shaking leaves to tunes on repeat,
Tiny roots moving to the beat.

With a twist and a playful spin,
This pot plant knows how to win.
A dance-off with the cactus next door,
Now that's a sight—who could ask for more?

Against the wall, a geranium prances,
While the herbs join in with wild glances.
They giggle, they sway, there's no restraint,
Even the orchids join in as faint.

So here's to the flora, bold and spry,
In pots they dance, reaching for the sky.
With each silly step and delightful prance,
These daring plants truly know how to dance.

Nature's Tenacity

A stubborn sprout in a chipped old pot,
Thinks it's a tree, oh what a thought!
Striving high, yet staying small,
Waving to the butterflies that call.

Beneath the sink, a fern looks grim,
"Watch me thrive!" it sings, though chances seem slim.
It stretches out with leafy arms,
Desperate for sunlight and garden charms.

A dandelion thinks itself a star,
On the windowsill, it dreams of afar.
"Look at me, I'm tough!" it shouts with glee,
While a nearby pansy just snorts in glee.

So cheers to the plants that laugh at fate,
With roots so deep, they're never late.
In pots so snug, they'll outlive the fuss,
Nature's fighters, they'll make a plus!

Dreams in a Pot

In a flower pot, dreams come alive,
A basil wishes it could jive.
Each night it fantasizes of a quilt,
While the thyme rolls over, feeling guilty.

An aloe hopes to join a band,
But knows in truth it can't withstand.
Imagining guitar riffs in the sun,
While ignoring its own lack of fun.

The mint dreams of dancing on the lawn,
But is stuck in its earthy dawn.
"What a life I'd lead," it whispers low,
If I could just find a place to grow!

Yet every pot holds a secret cheer,
Making the most of its cozy sphere.
With dreams alight and hopes so free,
In their little world, just let them be!

Singing Without Sun

In shadows deep, a plant holds tight,
Singing ballads into the night.
"Where's the sun?" it laments with flair,
Crooning to the spider spinning near.

With no light to fuel its growing art,
It enlists the moon to play its part.
Together they make a curious tune,
Of mimicked rays and evening's boon.

"Come join me!" calls a timid sage,
"With no beams around, we'll create our stage!"
So leaves start swaying, harmony flows,
A midnight concert for all who know.

So here they thrive, though light's in jail,
In soft shadows, they still set sail.
Singing sweet songs, they have their fun,
Proving life can thrive, even without sun!

A Secret Garden Within

In corners of chaos, plants start to grow,
A cactus in the bathroom, putting on a show.
My laundry's a jungle, with vines now entwined,
Who knew that my socks could be so well-defined?

The fridge hides a sprout, all green and so bright,
It jokes with the leftovers, 'You're not a delight!'
A fern in the corner says, 'Chill, I'm your bud,'
I wink at the weeds, 'You're misunderstood!'

Stars Amidst the Smog

In the city's glow, where the stars like to hide,
I plant tiny dreams in the soot they provide.
A daisy on the rooftop shouts, 'Hey look at me!'
'Your high-flying ambitions smell more like a tree.'

My balcony's cluttered, it's a critter's retreat,
With pots full of herbs and a squirrel with a tweet.
He claims he's the king, I just roll my two eyes,
'In my minty palace, we'll feast on surprise!'

Heartfelt Growth

In this quirky old pot, a miracle starts,
With a smile and a giggle, they bloom from the hearts.
The tulips gossip, 'Look at Jeff, isn't he grand?'
But the roses just moan, 'He's not long for this land.'

I water my worries, add sunshine for cheer,
A snail on the rim says, 'Life's slow but sincere.'
With every small sprout, my spirit takes flight,
Who knew that a plant could be a friend overnight?

Life's Unlikely Endeavors

In a garden of dreams, the oddest things thrive,
A potato in flippers says, 'I'm glad to arrive!'
With carrots in tutus, they dance in a line,
'Life's too short for drudgery—join our fun design!'

A sprout with a top hat declares, 'What a sight!'
'We're thriving in chaos, and feeling just right.'
So here's to the laughter in potting our woes,
Life's truly a party, as any seed knows!

The Art of Surviving Tight Spaces

In this cramped little pot, I stand tall,
My neighbor's a weed, can I scale that wall?
I stretch out my leaves, I dance and I sway,
Who knew that this spot would make my day?

The sun glints on me, I'm quite the sight,
I play peek-a-boo with the morning light.
Though squeezed in here, I won't be a bore,
I'll spin a tale of triumph galore!

With roots intertwined, we share all the fun,
In our limited space, we'll outshine the sun.
So here's to the petals, we'll color the air,
Two peas in a pod, beyond compare!

So laugh with me now, let's cheer for our fate,
In a tiny little world, we'll still celebrate.
Though bound by the pot, we'll reach for the sky,
And giggle at limits, oh my, oh my!

Sowing Light in the Gloom

In shadows I sprout and try to be bright,
Who knew I'd be stuck where the sun fears to fight?
I chat with the gloom, we're the best of pals,
With humor and joy, we throw grand galas!

I wiggle my leaves just to see what they say,
A pun a day keeps the darkness at bay.
The sun's on a break, but I'm still having fun,
Planting my smiles, I'm the cheeky one!

With roots deep in soil, I refuse to sulk,
Even in shade, I've a playful smile, and bulk.
Elbows with crickets, we dance in this gloom,
Together we plot, a bright future to loom!

So wave your hands high, my delightfully frail friends,
We'll sow all the laughter that never quite ends.
For even in darkness, our spirits can rise,
With giggles and chuckles, we'll light up the skies!

Flourishing in Fragility

I'm delicate, sure, but I'll frolic and sway,
In this flimsy old pot, I'm having my way.
Each petal is laughter, each leaf is a cheer,
Who said being fragile is something to fear?

I teeter and totter, a dance on the edge,
With roots just a whisper, I'd still make a pledge.
To flaunt all my petals, to sprinkle some joy,
Even the wind can't dull this good ol' ploy!

With every slight breeze, I'm a giggling sprite,
Tickled by danger, I'm ready to fight.
My frailty's my charm, in a quirky ballet,
I'll twirl through the chaos, come what may!

So here's to the soft, the meek and the small,
We'll dance in the breezes and rise after the fall.
In every mishap, there's laughter to find,
Flourishing wildly, a whimsical mind!

Hope Takes Root

In the heart of the chaos, I dig down my toes,
Sowing seeds of laughter where nobody goes.
With optimism sprouting, I wiggle and giggle,
Hoping to thrive in a little pot wiggle!

Time to sprout funny tales of my plight,
When others see darkness, I bask in the light.
For colors of hope dance upon my small leaves,
In this little old pot where no one believes!

With every new dawn, I stretch for the sky,
Sharing smiles with clouds as they drift by.
Though stunted in size, I won't sell my soul,
I'm a hopeful little sprout playing my role!

So let's raise a toast to the roots in our hearts,
In spaces so tight, we'll still play our parts.
With hope as our sunshine, we'll happily grow,
In this funny little plot, we'll steal the show!

Life from a Small Seed

In a tiny pot, I make my stand,
With dreams so big, like a marching band.
I wiggle and jiggle in my cramped space,
Each leaf a grin, on my little face.

Neighbors nearby, they roll their eyes,
But I'm growing tall, much to their surprise.
With sunshine smiles, I stretch and sway,
Turning their frowns into laughter, hooray!

Roots dancing deep beneath the soil,
While I germinate joy with quirks and toil.
Though I may be small, my heart is grand,
In this little patch, I take command.

So here I stay, no need to roam,
In this cozy pot, I've found my home.
Watch me flourish, I'll give you a show,
A spectacle here, a seed's version of a glow.

Flourishing in the Forgotten

In a dusty corner, I've planted my time,
With pots of laughter, I'm growing sublime.
While others get sunlight, I dance in the shade,
Creating my beauty, no plans to evade.

Ignored by the world, I wave with glee,
Every little bloom a joyful decree.
Who needs the limelight, when you've got flair?
I'm thriving in silence, without a care.

Cacti and ferns all gather around,
To share in my antics, oh, what a sound!
With every odd glance, I simply wink,
In this quiet spot, I'm the link.

So here I thrive, in this barely-known nook,
Crafting my laughter in every little crook.
When life forgets you, don't hide or shrink,
Sing in your silence, let them all think!

Hope in a Restricted Plot

In a box of wood, I wiggle and cheer,
Despite the small space, I've got no fear.
With tiny twists and a brave little shout,
I'll take what I've got and turn it about.

Directionless dreams? Not in my plan,
I'll stretch out my leaves, be the funnier man.
With roots intertwined, we'll hold a surprise,
When they see the magic, oh, how they'll rise!

Locked in a space, they think I'm confined,
But in my small world, new wonders I find.
With each little petal in my own quirky plot,
I'm the hopeful spirit that can't be forgot.

So watch me grow tall, it's a deliberate scheme,
In every constraint, I'll craft a new dream.
With humor and joy, I'll sow my delight,
In this restricted plot, let my charm take flight.

Radiance in Restraint

In a pot just tight, I shine like the sun,
With a spirit so bright, I'm ready for fun.
Bound by the edges, but laughter can spread,
Sipping on sunshine, with joy in my head.

Here's a leaf waving, with cheer and delight,
In my cozy corner, I'm winning this fight.
I've learned from the soil, from the warmth and the gloom,
To twirl out my colors, making my room.

Constraints are a giggle in my little parade,
I strut and I stand, with no grand charade.
With blossoms so bold that shake off the dust,
I turn every limit to laughter and trust.

So here I will twirl, in this space that's my own,
Radiant and rich, not just overgrown.
With humor my garden, in width or in height,
I flaunt my spirit, a dazzling sight!

From Seedling to Spectacle

I started as a seed in a little cup,
With dreams of the sky and a wish to erupt.
But here I am stuck with a view of my toes,
Still, I'll dance and shake in my pot like a pro.

My leaves are quite modest, my flowers a tease,
Yet I wiggle and laugh with the greatest of ease.
While others may soar like a bird on the wing,
I'll twirl in my spot, oh, the joy that I bring!

The sun's blazing down with a smirk in its rays,
And I'm just here sipping on sunlight all day.
I trade lofty heights for a patch on the floor,
But I'm happy to shine; oh, who could want more?

So here's to my pot, it's a tiny domain,
Where I turn all my quirks into my own kind of fame.
With laughter and cheer, I connect with the dirt,
From seedling to spectacle, no reason to hurt!

Radiance from Restraint

Oh, I'm potted tight, like a sardine in a can,
Yet I stretch and I reach, yes, that's my grand plan!
While others may frolic in fields full of space,
I charm all my neighbors with a smile on my face.

The confines are cozy, snug as a bug,
With roots wrapped up tight and still full of snug.
I'll gossip with daisies, gossip with thyme,
And throw in a joke that does humor sublime.

With sunshine as my buddy, I shrug off the fuss,
I dance with the shadows, just me and my rust!
Restraint? What a concept! I'll spin and I'll twirl,
In this pot of mine, I'm still the queen of my world!

So cheers to the boundaries, I'll raise my green cups,
For within these four walls, oh, I'm filling them up!
With laughter and light, I toast to this state,
In the realm of constraints, I'm still feeling great!

Growth within Confines

Confined in a pot, who knew I could shine?
With roots all tangled but I'm feeling divine!
I may lack the vista, the expanse of a field,
Yet my quirky green charm is a treasure concealed.

They chuckle and snicker, "Oh, look at that sprout!"
But I'll throw them a grin, "You should check me out!"
For growth can be sneaky, it doesn't need ground,
In a tiny old planter, joy can abound!

I'll swap tales with basil, hold court with a weed,
In this miniature kingdom, there's plenty to heed.
Each petal a punchline, each stem a big laugh,
In a pot of delight, oh, how I'm the chaff!

So here's to the limits, I'm raising my cheer,
In my little world, there's no reason for fear.
I may be a potted plant with roots quite confined,
But you'll find I'm a riot, and oh so refined!

The Heart of a Wildflower

Here I sit in a pot, a wild spirit at heart,
With dreams of the meadow, that's just how I start.
I daydream of prairies and jewels in the grass,
But for now, I'll just giggle and let this time pass.

I wear blooms like a crown, though my home's a small jar,
And I'm twirling with glee, feeling like a rockstar!
The world may be narrow, but my spirit's a blaze,
With jokes and antics that'll surely amaze!

When the wind tickles petals, I dance on my perch,
My roots may be cramped, but I'm never in search.
The heart of a wildflower is free as can be,
Stuck in a pot, but oh, can't you see?

So here's to my antics, my joy unconfined,
In this little container, I'm still unrefined.
I'll spread laughter and colors, a floral delight,
The heart of a wildflower shining so bright!

Leafing Out in Darkness

In pots too dark, I start to sprout,
With no sunlight, I still shout.
Who needs the rays when I can dance?
This leafy life is quite a chance.

My roots are tangled in the clay,
No need for sun, I'm here to stay.
With every twist, I find my way,
Feeling like a plant in a cabaret.

No need for fuss or fancy soil,
I'll grow through grime, I'll never spoil.
With laughter in the wilted air,
I'll be the fern with the flair to spare.

So bring on shadows, bring on gloom,
I'll still be thriving from this room.
In darkness, I'll shake and sway,
Who knew plants could party this way?

Vibrancy in Veiled Spaces

In corners dark, I claim my throne,
A little light, and I'm not alone.
Waving leaves of every hue,
Sunbeam dodging, what's a plant to do?

I sport my dust like a badge of pride,
In hidden spots, I'll never hide.
With a giggle at the grimmest sight,
I'm the wild one in the dim twilight.

My colors pop like birthday cake,
While everyone else is still asleep.
A party plant, that's who I am,
In little nooks, I flash and glam.

You'll find me where the shadows creep,
Giggling soft while others weep.
A vibrant force that won't unwind,
In veiled spaces, I'm one of a kind!

Whispers of Wildness

Potted snugly, I whisper loud,
I'm the wildflower in the crowd.
In cramped quarters, I still roam,
My leaves are tales of a traveled home.

With every breeze, I spread my cheer,
Who knew a plant could be so dear?
I'll shimmy and shake in pots so tight,
A little wildness feels just right.

Sprouting dreams in a tiny cup,
Watch me twist and flip, oh what's up?
While others fret about their space,
I'll dance like I'm at a big old race.

So here I stand, in my leafy dress,
With petals bright, I'm here to impress.
In whispers of wildness, I'll ignite,
A riot of color, what a delight!

Transcending the Limits

If pots confine me, I'll break the mold,
With roots so feisty, a sight to behold.
No ceiling high can hold me down,
I'm the jester in this garden town.

I'm climbing walls, I'm stretching wide,
Exploring heights with leafy pride.
While others shrink in fear of height,
I'll juggle clouds, it's sheer delight.

In terracotta, I'll make my mark,
With every inch, I'll leave my spark.
No limits here, I'll sing and shout,
Just watch me play, there's no doubt.

So cheers to pots where we can thrive,
In every nook, we feel alive.
Transcending borders with every spray,
A playful plant, I'll lead the way!

Life's Stride in a Small Circle

In this tiny patch I tread,
With daisies poking at my head.
I spin around, what a sight,
A flower dance, in pure delight.

The ants march by, in straight lines,
While I'm just here, drinking brine.
A squirrel snickers at my prance,
As I engage in my own dance.

I stretch my limbs, I wave my hands,
I'm the king of these small lands.
A dandelion's my trusty steed,
In an adventure I didn't heed.

So here I stay, still having fun,
Just watch me shine, a big-eyed sun.
In a pot, I'll live my dream,
For who needs space, when you can beam?

Grit and Grace

With grit, I sprout from asphalt grey,
A noble quest, come what may.
Though squirrels mock my dream so bold,
I stand my ground, with glints of gold.

A chipmunk yells, "You're just a weed!"
I wink and say, "Yes, but I lead!"
I twist, I turn, with poise and flair,
Each sunrise brings a new affair.

My roots may tangle, my leaves may bend,
But here I thrive, no need to pretend.
With laughter loud, and jokes to share,
I flaunt my beauty, without a care.

So sip your tea, and watch me grow,
In this little plot, I steal the show.
With grit and grace, I'll take my chance,
Dancing here in my own little prance.

Unfolding Among the Unlikely

In a pot with a broken rim,
I wave my stems, I spread my whim.
Surrounded by things that should not be,
I'm the wildflower, can't you see?

With pruners near, they plot my doom,
But I just giggle, and make some room.
The marigold shrugs, unsure of me,
But I'll make us friends, wait and see!

A gopher sneaks, thinking it's grand,
But I have roots, and a brave stand.
With every poke and playful tease,
I grow more strong, do as I please!

So if you doubt my little gig,
Take a seat and watch me dig.
In this odd crowd, I'll find my place,
Unfolding softly with a silly grace.

A Garden in Quarters

Welcome, friends, to my small zone,
In just three feet, I've found my throne.
With herbs and blooms so brightly clad,
In this snug plot, it's never bad.

Petunias giggle, while veggies chatter,
About the things that truly matter.
A misfit crew, we share a laugh,
As the sunlight lights up our path.

The radishes plan a culinary show,
While thymes recite poetry on the go.
Squashed between onions and thyme,
We paint the air with colors and rhyme.

So join the fun in my garden tight,
With every leaf, our spirits take flight.
In this playful patch, with laughter sweet,
Life is grand, in this cozy seat.

Unyielding in the Cracks

In the sidewalk there's a sprout,
It drinks rain, what's that about?
No garden bed, it laughs instead,
Spreading joy where weeds dread.

A kitty hops, it gives a stare,
"What's that green thing? Looks quite rare!"
With each inch, it sways with glee,
"Here I am, just wait and see!"

Concrete's harsh, but here I stand,
With my little leafy hand.
Dancing bright, dodging the shoe,
I'm a superstar, who are you?

Sidewalk's home, I wear it proud,
In a crack, I draw a crowd.
Take that, soil! You think you're slick?
I'll show you I can grow, quick!

Awakening the Unseen

Underneath the rustling leaves,
A tiny bud just plots and weaves.
It dreams of worlds beyond the pot,
With sunlit visions it's forgot.

The snooty daisies raise an eye,
"Who's that brave soul? So spry, oh my!"
With roots like magic, twisted, quirky,
It just smiles, feeling perky!

The garden's guard? A gnome in fright,
"Dear plant, don't plan to take your flight!"
But up it stretches, giggles abound,
"I'll make my mark without a mound!"

So here I wait, a sprightly jest,
In pots, I'll put my humor to test.
Watch me thrive in this confined space,
With charm and sass, I win the race!

The Flourish of the Unbound

In a can of beans, a flower peeks,
"Surprise!" it shouts, it hardly speaks.
With eyes so wide, it starts to sway,
"Who needs soil? I'll rule the day!"

A cactus joins with prickly taunt,
"Hey man, that's quite the odd front!"
"It's called style," the flower blares,
"Hope you don't mistake me for chairs!"

Fans of potting? Not my scene,
In a flip-flop, I'll reign supreme!
With laughter loud and petals bold,
I'm the tale that's yet untold!

So bring your pots, and bring your plans,
I'll show you how to dance with cans!
In fields of metal and cardboard too,
I'll sprinkle joy in shades of blue!

Courage to Thrive

A sprout in want of space to twirl,
Dreams of sunshine, gives a whirl.
It flicks aside the dirt and grime,
"I'll wear my petals, that's the rhyme!"

In a corner near the bustling street,
A dandelion with quite the beat.
"Who needs a garden?" it smirks with flair,
"Just me and my friends—fresh air to share!"

A flowerpot with lots of hope,
Gave a gnome some serious scope.
Holding tight, it knows the score,
"Let's dance in shades of green galore!"

So here's to plants that brave the jest,
In wacky places, they find their quest.
With spirits high, against the odds,
They laugh and grow—applaud the gods!

Embracing the Unfamiliar Soil

In a pot too small for dreams,
I dance with roots, or so it seems.
The sun might whisper, "Go get lost!"
But here I thrive, no matter the cost.

A bit of dirt, a bit of light,
I wiggle and jiggle, what a delight!
With neighbors like cacti, sharp and tall,
I play my tunes, not scared at all.

With water from a melted ice,
I sip and grin, oh, isn't life nice?
The gardener stares, confused, aghast,
While I sprout tales of the wild past.

So here I am, in this tiny plot,
Making the most of what I've got.
Unfamiliar soil? It's a grand surprise,
Just watch me thrive while others sigh.

Petals Amidst the Pavement

Amidst the cracks, I raise my head,
With sidewalk grit, my dreams are spread.
A flower in sneakers, watch me prance,
In this concrete jungle, I'll take my chance.

The traffic roars, but I sing loud,
A floral riot, oh so proud!
Dandelions giggle, and daisies cheer,
While pigeons stare, bewildered in fear.

A petal here, a petal there,
Spreading joy with the sidewalk flair.
Who needs a garden, with daisies that pop?
I'm the charm of this bustling shop.

So join my stroll on this busy street,
Together we'll dance to a summer beat.
Sprouting laughter from urban gloom,
In the cracks of the pavement, I find my bloom.

Cultivating Beauty in Constraint

In a vase constrained, I twirl around,
With just a splash, I'm beauty bound.
No garden gate can hold me tight,
I flourish among the kitchen light.

The fridge hums songs of pickles and pies,
While I sway gently, oh what a prize!
No room to roam, but who needs the grass?
In my glass jail, let the laughter amass.

Chives might roll their eyes at my flair,
But I'm the star, simply beyond compare.
Little buds giggle, no worries on sight,
In constraints we dance, what pure delight.

With sunlight streaming through the glass pane,
I wave good morning to the passing rain.
So let them snicker, I'll just stay spry,
Growing wild, where dreams can fly.

Growing Through Grit

In the harshest soil, I dig and strive,
With grit and giggles, I come alive.
The winds may howl, the storms may roar,
But I'm the flower who asks for more.

My petals may bend, but they won't break,
I laugh in the face of each mistake.
With roots so deep, I hold on tight,
Dancing through darkness, swaying with light.

Every bruise tells a story, oh so grand,
Of battles fought and hope at hand.
Compost dreams mean I'm never alone,
In grit we trust; the world is our throne.

So if you find life tough as nails,
Just think of me, with my vibrant trails.
Through laughter and grit, together we'll grow,
In the wildest places, we put on a show.

Cherishing Every Inch

In a tiny pot, I wiggle with glee,
Roots go wild, feeling quite free.
Sunshine or shade, I thrive in the space,
Who knew I could grow in such a small place?

Watch me stretch on this sunny little shelf,
Taking my selfies, oh, what a stealth!
Neighboring cacti give me the glare,
But I just smile, without a care.

Surging Through the Cracks

Cracks in the sidewalk, my stage for the day,
With swagger and style, I dance and sway.
Pavement, you thought you could keep me down?
But here I am, the queen of this town!

Petunias and daisies laugh at my zest,
But I'm just a weed, I don't need their jest!
Each crack is a party, an open invite,
To stretch out my petals, let's light up the night.

The Quiet Strength of Growth

I quietly rise from a pot full of grit,
With just a few leaves, I'll muster a wit.
Neighbors don't notice, they're all in a rush,
But here I'm preparing, with nary a hush!

In shadows I linger, with dreams to ignite,
Plotting my journey, from morning to night.
Watch as I flourish and take them by storm,
With every small inch, I break out of norm.

Flourishing in the Fissures

Fissures and rocks can't keep me at bay,
While others complain, I'm ready to play.
With laughter and joy, I'll surprise and delight,
A bloom on a rubble, such a wondrous sight!

I tickle their fancies as I reach for the sky,
While grumpy old weeds just sigh and ask why.
I'll dance in my pot, do my own silly jig,
In this garden of life, I'll be the big gig!

Green Among the Gray

In a concrete jungle, I stand so bright,
Wishing the pigeons would take a flight.
With my plastic leaves and sunlight glow,
I'm the envy of all in this boring show.

Wiggling my roots in this tiny pot,
Making friends with the dust bunnies, quite a lot.
Laughing at mops and their sweeping woes,
While I sip on sunlight, in fabulous clothes.

They complain of the gloom, the skies so bleak,
But here in my corner, I'm quite the freak.
Stylin' with color, my petals are loud,
Who knew being green could attract such a crowd?

So raise a glass to the weeds and the grass,
We're the life of the party, let's make it last!
In a world of dullness, we break the mold,
Life's a little funnier when you're bright and bold.

Defying the Nest

Tucked in a corner, I giggle and sway,
Challenging norms in a quirky display.
The pot may be small, but my dreams are grand,
Breaking the rules with a green little band.

The birds think they're clever, perched up so high,
But I've got my roots, and I'm reaching the sky.
I don't need their heights, or their lofty view,
I'm cozied in dirt, and I'm loving it too!

When the sun beams down, I twirl and I dance,
Making my moments a whimsical chance.
Every droplet of rain gives a giggle or two,
Bring on the storms, I'll tango with dew!

While others complain, I'm soaking it in,
The fun is afoot, let the merriment begin!
So here's to the greenies, who know how to nest,
We're not just surviving, we're living our best!

Vibrancy in a Vessel

Inside this pot, I declare my reign,
With paint by the flowers, I'll never be plain.
The neighbors are dull, stuck in their gray,
But my petals throw parties every single day!

When rain clouds gather in skies full of gloom,
I throw confetti, it's my little room.
The world may be boring, but I've got flair,
Dancing with shadows, without a care!

I've got my own style, it's flashy and new,
Sprouting wild thoughts, in every shade and hue.
A dash of the wacky, a sprinkle of fun,
I brighten the day with a wink and a pun.

So here's to the pot, my home sweet home,
Where laughter and colors are free to roam.
I may be contained, but my spirit's so free,
In this crazy vessel, you'll always find me!

Cultivating Joy in the Mundane

From morning to evening, I soak up the sun,
Spreading my joy, oh isn't it fun?
In everyday soil, I find delight,
Even when shadows try to steal my light.

The humans hurry, lost in their race,
While I stretch my leaves with a leisurely grace.
When life's in a rush, I sit back and grin,
For laughter and sunshine are always my win!

With a sip of fresh rain, I chuckle and cheer,
Making buckets of joy in a measured sphere.
Spreading the whimsies, like petals on air,
Finding the giggles in dust and despair.

So here's to the moments, both simple and bright,
Cultivating laughter, with all of my might.
In the mundane we find our unique little song,
So join me, dear friend, let's dance all day long!

Strength in Smallings

In a pot that's quite snug,
I wiggle and jiggle with glee.
Roots so tiny, but oh, what a hug,
I dance with the breeze, feeling free.

Sunshine laughs, and raindrops sing,
Little leaves waving, what a scene!
I might be small, but I'm full of zing,
In this cozy home, I'm the queen!

The Power of Patience

They planted me here in a cup,
Waiting for growth, quite the tease!
Each day I stretch, not giving up,
Just sipping the dew with such ease.

Those big blooms strut, oh what a sight,
But I know I'll get my own chance.
With a bit of sunshine, pure delight,
Tiny wonders can also dance!

Tenacity in Tiny Pots

In this narrow space, I thrive,
Bouncing back with every shower.
While others grow tall and dive,
I'm a champion of the lower flower.

Might take time, but I've got the flair,
Catch me grinning, no need to pout.
It's a pot of laughter in the air,
Believe me, I'm what it's about!

The Spirit of Survival

Life's a ride in this little home,
Battling weeds and pests galore.
Yet with a chuckle, I can comb,
Finding sunshine is what I adore.

From cracks in the sidewalk, I might peep,
With roots that tickle and plot.
Each day's an adventure, oh so deep,
In my tiny world, I'm quite hot!

Courageous Petals

In the crack of a sidewalk, a dandelion grins,
Waving 'hello' to passersby with wins.
"I might be a weed, but I'm a sight to see,"
Sassy and sun-kissed, just wild and free.

Beneath the big rocks, where no one would dare,
A daisy stands tall with flowers in hair.
"Look at me now, in this impossible spot!"
I'm not in the garden, but I give it a shot!

A cactus in sneakers, with swagger it poses,
"Who needs a pot when you've got funky roses?"
With thorns and a grin, it shares its keen sense,
"Life's what you make it, no need for pretense!"

And so they all flourish, in odd places found,
Making a ruckus, they dance all around.
Their vibrant defiance in laughter, it grows,
Watch out for weeds, they're stealing the show!

The Tenacious Tapestry

A patch of wildflowers, bright under the sun,
Cheerfully shouting, "We're just having fun!"
Ragged and rugged, with charm they will sway,
"We're the stars of the garden, so step out of the way!"

With bees on their tails, they hustle and twirl,
"Look out, world! You're in for a whirl!"
They spread their bright laughter; pollen in the air,
"Catch us if you can! We just don't care!"

A sunflower struts, with its head held up high,
"You think I'm just tall? Just watch as I fly!"
With each little breeze, it leans and it bends,
Life's a full-blown party—who needs to pretend?

In cracks of the pavement, they lay down their beat,
Every squished little stem still finds life to repeat.
So come join the fun in this playful parade,
Where nothing can stop us—we won't be dismayed!

Color in Grey Spaces

In a town dressed in grey, a flower stood proud,
"I'm not just a speck, I'm a colorful crowd!"
With petals of pink, and a wink of bright blue,
It chuckled and coaxed, "Come join in, won't you?"

A wallflower smirked with its bold polka dots,
"Grey's nice and all, but it needs some hot shots!"
With flair and with pizzazz, it jumped in the game,
"Life's a canvas, not just a frame!"

The roses vied hard for their moments of fame,
"Let's paint it with fragrance, we're not all the same!"
In a city of monotones, they twirled with delight,
Spinning joy from the dull, they felt so right.

Every nook, every cranny, they filled it with cheer,
Thus out of the shadows, they conquered the fear.
In the most unexpected, they'd sing and they'd sway,
Adding color to moments in a dazzling way!

Stories of the Unsheltered

In a concrete jungle, a weed weaves a tale,
"I may not have roots, but I sure won't fail!"
With laughter and grit, it spins yarns through the air,
"Life's not all perfect, but I'm still the flair!"

A tulip once whispered, full of clumsy grace,
"I've danced in the rain with a smile on my face!"
"So what if I falter? I'm proud and I'm bright,
These adventures I cherish, my joy is my right!"

An acorn once joked, with dreams in its trunk,
"I'm not just a nut; I'm an oak, don't be punked!"
With dreams like the skyline, they reach for the stars,
In every mishap, they laugh at their scars.

So here's to the stories of those who just thrive,
In places aimed low, oh, they feel so alive!
For every small sprout in the wild, hear it bold,
Lives full of laughter are worth more than gold!

Garden of the Boundless Heart

In a pot of dirt, I sit quite snug,
Hoping for sunlight, but get a hug.
The neighbors think I'm quite unkempt,
But I'm the wild one, no need for preempt.

My leaves are tangled, my roots in a twist,
Yet I'm making friends with the evening mist.
A flower power party, I plan to host,
With weeds as the bouncers, they'll get the most.

I'll dance with the snails, confetti of dust,
Gossip with the ants, in worms we trust.
My petals might sag, my charm's still bright,
Catch me in a pot, reveling in delight.

So here in my vessel, I lift my leaf,
Frolicking with joy, hanging on a brief.
You can keep your gardens, all green and grand,
I've got my own party, just watch me expand!

Sunshine in Shaded Corners

In a nook of gloom, I found my cheer,
Sunshine peeks in, gives me a smirk.
Behind the curtain, I wiggle and sway,
Nothing stops me from having my day.

I stretch and reach for the light's warm embrace,
Dodging the dust bunnies, I'm winning this race.
The cat thinks I'm odd, a funny old gal,
But I laugh in the shade, quite the herbal pal.

My leaves joke around, they tickle the air,
Whispering secrets, like none would dare.
I'm thriving in corners, where others would pout,
Here's to the shade, I bloom without doubt!

A party of shadows, with flickers of gold,
Tales of a plant that is bright and bold.
So light up your spaces, don't fret about strife,
I found my own sunshine, and I'm living my life!

Vibrant Hues from Small Spaces

In the smallest of pots, I throw a fit,
Colors galore, with every little bit.
Saturated dreams in a tiny abode,
Unleashing my joy on this dinky road.

A splatter of petals, in chaos I thrive,
Artists call me 'messy,' but I'm so alive!
With stickers and sprinkles, my canvas is bright,
Who needs a meadow? I'm a garden of light.

Each leaf is a rebel, with quirks all its own,
Together we giggle at how we have grown.
"Small but fierce," we chant, as the bees swarm around,
In this little patch, happiness is found.

So let the garden book tell you are small,
In reality, we're having ourselves a ball.
Tiny is mighty, it's positively clear,
In vibrant hues, I'm the champion here!

Unfurling Dreams in Tight Quarters

Stuck in this space, I feel quite confined,
But dreams have no bounds—just look what I find!
A daisy with sass, and a rose with a grin,
Together we're dancing, under this skin.

A cocktail of colors, we sip on the sun,
Sprinkled with laughter, we're having such fun.
Tight quarters are cozy, our spirits run free,
Here's to the chaos, come dance with me!

I throw out my petals, no space to hold back,
Making my mark on this floral attack.
We might be small, but we're bold and we cheer,
In our tight little realm, there's nothing to fear.

So next time you see, a plant looking frail,
Remember our hearts, they'll never grow pale.
Unfurling our dreams, we take on the world,
In tight little pots, our identities swirled!

From Seed to Surreal

In a pot which is much too small,
Danced a sprout, feeling quite tall.
Said, "I'll grow, despite the squeeze!"
And dreams of sunshine teased a breeze.

With roots that tangled and cursed the space,
Offered a show of the silliest grace.
Wiggled and jiggled, a true superstar,
"Who needs vast fields? I'd rather be bizarre!"

They called it absurd, a rib-tickling sight,
A daisy in a jug, oh what a delight!
"Watch me thrive in this cozy lap,
As I sip my dew and take a nap!"

From seed to surreal, a quirky quest;
Proving that small can truly be best.
With laughter and light, this tale unfolds,
In a world where joy, like magic, beholds.

Overcoming Barriers

A cactus dreamed of a beachy scene,
But found itself stuck between washing machines.
"I need some sand, not this cold metal!"
But found mirth amidst the battle of petals.

With spines that poked at the laundry pile,
"I'm not a lamp! I'm a cactus with style!"
It wore a hat made of dryer sheets,
Creating the funniest of beach retreats.

The neighbors giggled, tears in their eyes,
As the cactus tried hard to rise and surprise.
"I'll sprout my own paradise right here,
In this chaotic coral of fluff and sheer!"

With dreams too big for its metal cage,
It laughed at limits, roaring with sage,
And ended up throwing the wildest bash,
With spin cycles twirling, what a splash!

The Journey of the Stalwart

A tiny weed with a giant heart,
Set out on a journey, ready to start.
"I won't be mowed! I'll stand with flair!"
With dirt in its roots and wind in its hair.

Past garden gnomes and flower beds bright,
It shouted, "I'll conquer, oh what a sight!"
With each twist and turn, a clever jest,
As bugs rolled with laughter, it felt so blessed.

Through busy roads and skateboard parks,
It sidestepped bikes, threw away the sparks.
"I'd rather grow tall near this old fence,
Than stay stagnant, playing defense!"

With resilience wrapped in a comical spree,
It danced in the breeze, wild and free.
For a weed can be bold, a hero unplanned,
Taking root wherever it can stand.

Shades of Resilience

In a pot of gray, under a dim light,
A flower sighed, "Not much of a sight!"
Yet it wore colors of the silliest hue,
With glittery petals, a dance to pursue.

It painted the pot with stripes and swirls,
Brought laughter to the drab, made heads twirl.
"Who says I can't shine in this small round space?
I'll catch your eye with a funky embrace!"

With every flop and fumble, it grinned,
"Resilience is key; let the fun begin!"
Making friends with a snoozing cat,
And promising joy in a colorful spat.

In shades of resilience, the laughter shared,
This quirky little flower had truly dared.
"I may be potted, but so full of cheer,
Watch me light up this room, yeah, that's my career!"

Nature's Quiet Epic

In the corner, a house plant waits,
Dreaming of vines and garden gates.
With sunlight streaming, it stretches wide,
Pretending it's on a wild joyride.

It shakes its leaves with all its might,
Hoping the neighbors witness its height.
While sipping dust from a pot so small,
It plots to outgrow the wall right tall.

A spider crawls with views so grand,
Gossiping 'bout growth throughout the land.
"Oh, to be outside!" the plant will cry,
As it waves a leaf to the fluttering fly.

Yet here it stands, content and snug,
While chubby cats give it a hug.
With every breeze, it pirouettes,
In this small kingdom, none have regrets.

Unexpected Harvests

In a pot on the sill, a potato sneers,
"I'll grow here just fine, despite your fears."
With eyes like jewels, and skin good as gold,
A rebel in soil, breaking the mold.

The neighbors will gasp when they find my prize,
A marvel of flora, a true surprise.
They all thought I'd rot, just a scrap on the floor,
But I'm planning a feast, and oh, there's more!

Carrots in shoes, dancing wildly around,
Softly giggling without a sound.
While mint takes the lead, with a jubilant sway,
Saying, "Let's have a party, come join the fray!"

From kitchen to pot, the laughter grows,
Each quirky plant flaunts its farmer knows.
In this tiny patch, hilarity thrives,
Unexpected harvests are how we survive!

Flourishing with Grace

A cactus struts with its prickly shoes,
Feeling the vibes, soaking up the views.
"Come close," it says, with a wink and a grin,
"I may have needles, but I'm soft within!"

With each little bloom, a giggle it wrangles,
It knows how to charm, despite all the tangles.
While ferns fawn over their silky fronds,
The cactus jests, skipping all the blondes.

Plants in the sun compose funny tales,
As peas plot schemes to escape their pails.
"Why settle for pots when there's dirt to explore?"
They moan and they giggle, then scatter for more.

So here's to the shrubs and wild little weeds,
Finding their fun, planting their seeds.
In corners of kitchens or basements a space,
All thrive with a laugh, just flourishing with grace!

Triumph of Nature's Spirit

A tiny flower claims its space,
Amidst the clutter, it's taking its place.
With petals bright and a cheeky stance,
It sings in the breeze, inviting a dance.

"Why must I wilt? I've got a plan!"
"To take the sun as a true green fan."
While weeds roll their eyes at the grandeur it fakes,
The flower just laughs, "For my tea, there's no stakes!"

A sprout on the windowsill feels so bold,
Challenging gravity, it dares to unfold.
Swinging its leaves while the cat's in a nap,
"Hey, check out my moves! I'm the king of this map!"

Victory squeaks from each leafy embrace,
As sprouts of all kinds twist with delight in their chase.
In pots or in gardens, we're here to incite,
The triumph of nature, let's bloom with delight!

www.ingramcontent.com/pod-product-compliance
Lightning Source LLC
Chambersburg PA
CBHW072118070526
44585CB00016B/1494